# Persuasion Mastery

The Ultimate Psychological Guide For Mind Control (Negotiation, Intuition, Body Language, Analysis)

Lance P. Richards

D1827237

Persuasion Mastery: The Ultimate Psychological Guide For Mind Control (Negotiation, Intuition, Body Language, Analysis)

# Table of Contents

# 1 - Introduction

I want to thank you and congratulate you for buying this book.

Persuasion is the art of convincing others to follow you or to do as you suggest. While this skill is important, most people do not study it. This is mostly due to the Machiavellian nature of the topic.

Regardless of what your view is on the topic, there is no doubt that it is essential for success. What you do with the skills you will learn in this book is up to you. Just be aware that by learning the skills offered here, you are gaining the powers that few men and women in history have mastered.

These skills were used by dictators in mobilizing entire countries. The same set of skills was used by men like Winston Churchill to serve the greater good. John F. Kennedy used these skills to convince America to go to the moon. At the other end of the spectrum, speeches of men like General Eisenhower and General Patton persuaded teens and young men to become warriors for their country.

The skill of controlling other people's actions is not just for the generals and presidents. Regardless of your occupation or your goals, you should learn how to persuade people because it is essential for success.

This skill can be applied to business, sales, law enforcement and in practicing law. Though not obvious, this skill could also be applied in multiple other industries. These skills can be applied when applying for a job or asking for a raise. They can also be used by managers and regular employees alike. It can be applied by students and educators. You can even apply the techniques herein managing your own family.

Regardless of what your goals are in life, you will need the skills that this book teaches. Just make sure to use this power responsibly.

Have I persuaded you to learn about persuasion?

Thank you for buying this book. I hope you enjoy it.

# 2 - The Power of Persuasion

We all know of people in our communities who seem to know how to get what they want from other people. When these people ask for something, we often give in. We have our individual reasons for doing so, but nevertheless, we give in.

These people have the power of persuasion. In most cases, we associate a person's ability to persuade to his or her power in our society. A person who can consistently persuade others is believed to not have difficult amassing more of the society's resources than his or her fair share.

Before moving on to the next paragraph, try to examine the society you are living in. Think of the influential people in your community and in your government. Ask yourself what these people have that make them so persuasive. Will you be able to replicate the qualities and assets that they have that make them persuasive?

## The Basics of Persuasion

Before we begin discussing the specific techniques for improving your persuasion skills, let us first discuss the meaning of persuasion. Persuasion refers to the ability to influence other people's actions. In its full glory, this power is masterfully used by politicians in getting the votes of the masses.

It is exhibited in how lobbyists get the votes of the people in the Congress to pass the bill that they need. It is shown in the ability of great generals to command their military personnel.

Persuasion, however, is not just practiced on the big stage. It also happens in everyday life. Every day, stores try to persuade you to come into their shops with big red signs in their windows. A neighbor may persuade you to go to their monthly dinner party. Your boss may persuade you to do better in the following month. A salesman may persuade you to buy a new car.

By learning how the power of persuasion operates, you will be able to avoid becoming victim to cheap tricks used by those who have mastered this skillset. With practice and the proper foundations set, you will also be able to master this power.

# You Need This Power to Reach Your Goals

Regardless of what you do or what your goals are, you will need the power of persuasion to get what you want. If you can persuade more people to work with you in achieving your goal, you will be able to reach that goal faster. Mastering this skill set will help you advance your career, improve your status in society, improve your financial situation and even make great and lasting changes in your society.

# This Power Requires Preparation

You cannot just wake up one morning, however, and begin persuading people. It does not work like that. This power requires a lot of preparation on your part. It requires you to build personal and social foundations. It also requires you to practice the skills required regularly.

If the goal that you want to achieve is great and the people you want to influence are stubborn, you will also need to plan your approach. In this book, we will discuss many skills and rules on how to be persuasive. It is up to you to choose the best method based on your goal and the people that you hope to persuade.

## 2 - THE POWER OF PERSUASION

In the next chapters, we will discuss the different personal and social skills that you need to build to increase your chances of success in persuading others.

# 3 - Learning the Basics of Making Deals

As you learn to be more persuasive, you will notice that no two negotiations are the same. Many factors make each deal or negotiation unique. If you want to succeed, you need to consider all the basic factors that affect these deals:

## The Target Audience

The target audience is always the first factor that you will always need to consider. Each person has a different opinion on how the deal should be made. Even people from the same companies, for instance, may think differently on their terms to complete the deal. To become successful in your future negotiations and deals, you need to analyze your target audience.

First, you need to make sure that you are dealing with the decision maker in the company or the group. In a standard company, you will notice that there is a hierarchy of power.

People in the higher echelons are usually more difficult to reach. Some of them are busy while others just have stubborn secretaries or assistants. You need to go through these gatekeepers before you can reach the decision maker.

## 3 - LEARNING THE BASICS OF MAKING DEALS

Once you have identified and reached the decision maker, you need to research and learn what their motivations are. When negotiating, you want to align your offer to the motivations of the target audience.

# 4 - The Offer

The offer for the deal is the second most important consideration. The offer refers to the goal (or purpose) that you want to get support for. The offer starts out as a goal. Most politicians, for instance, want to win their respective elections. On the other hand, a sales person's goal is to close a deal or make a sale.

Once the goal for the negotiations has been established, the next step is to transform the goal into an offer. To do this, you need to highlight what you want the target audience to do. In sales, for instance, most salespeople are pretty straightforward that they want you to buy their product or pay for their service.

Aside from this part of the offer, you should also add the reason for making the deal and how the target audience will benefit is they agree with you. In a sales pitch, this part is called the value proposition. It is normally used to make the target audience understand what they are getting into.

This is the factor where you are most likely to meet resistance from the target audience. If the target audience does not like the offer and the benefits, they can either walk away or negotiate to make the deal cover the terms that they want.

When the target audience is not contented with the offer, it is your job to keep them in the negotiation table and keep the deal alive. At this point, you could either agree to the terms that they ask for, add value to the offer unrelated to the terms or convince the target audience that they should take the offer the way it is.

## Giving in to their terms

When negotiating, you sometimes need to show that you are willing to compromise just to make the deal a reality. This is especially effective when you are dealing with competitive individuals. If the target audience sees the deal as a way to outsmart you, then the best way to close the deal is by making them think that they won.

You will need to take some safeguards when establishing the deal to make sure that it still covers your own goals. In sales, for example, you still need to consider the profits you stand to get if you will agree to a compromise. If there is no profit to be made, then the deal will not be successful even if it is closed.

# Adjusting the offer by adding an unrelated value

The next option for you when the target audience is not contented with the offer is to add value to the offer. Stores often do this by adding freebies when their customers make a purchase.

The 'free' item makes your target think that the deal is more valuable than it is. It also makes your offer more viable than your closest competitor. The freebie also puts you in a better position to distract the target audience from things they didn't agree with in the deal.

# Convince the target to take the deal as it is

The third option is probably the most difficult to pull off if the people you are dealing with find your offer wanting. If you are forced to take this option, the best thing to do is use the special tricks in this book to boost your chances of closing the deal.

Acknowledge the issues that the target audience has with the offer. You should also make them understand why these factors are essential to the deal.

After that, you need to look for an argument that will make them think that your offer is the best option they have. For instance, you can let them know that no other offer is better on the market today. If you can also compare the offer to its competition in the market, it would be helpful.

While this is the option that leads to most failed deals, it is sometimes necessary to stand your ground and stick with your initial offer.

## Your Negotiation Methods

Most of the things that will be discussed in this book will revolve around the methods that you can use when in the process of negotiating and the psychological and sociological basis for them.

You need to choose the methods carefully when negotiating to ensure success. It is important to make the offer enticing so that your target audience grabs it. They need to come to an understanding that it will be advantageous on their part if they follow your advice.

Executing the correct method will allow you to highlight the positive features of the offer or even the deal in general. It will boost the chances of success while making the target think that they are making the right choice.

Other factors that your target considers:

## The Competition

When creating the offer, anticipate what your competitor is offering the target audience.

In sales, the competition is easily identified. However, for other types of negotiations, rivals (or competitors) do not usually come out in the open. You can only be aware of it if your target audience gives you information that they already talked to some people offering similar deals.

If you can get hold of the information ahead of time, then you can make a better counter offer. Hence, it is imperative that you study your rivals (or competitors) so that you'll have an idea how they work.

## Your Confidence

Aside from the observable factors when presenting a deal, you also need to consider that your audience will also look for intangible factors to help them arrive at a decision. For one, they will be looking at how confident you are while presenting the deal, and with the goal in general.

Confidence is contagious. If your audience senses your conviction and deep belief in the offer and in yourself, they will trust you and eventually take your offer.

The people you are persuading will judge your confidence based on multiple factors including your voice, your choice of words, your posture, gestures and even the way you answer questions. Showing confidence in these aspects will significantly increase your chances of successfully persuading them.

# 5 - Start with Yourself

The first step in building your foundational skills to become persuasive is to work on yourself. Masters of persuasion are also experts on how they present themselves towards other people.

Powerful people know the effects of the impressions they make on their ability to persuade. A person dressed as a homeless man, for example, is not likely to persuade you to vote for him as the city mayor. Humans rely heavily on the sense of sight to judge the character of other people. While this is a common bias, you should use it to your advantage.

## Dress Like Popular Influential People

People of influence in your community have figured out the type of look that makes people look up to them. For instance, they try to maintain their hygiene, keep their hair groomed and dress appropriately according to the occasion. You should also do the same.

Remember that first impressions always last. When you are meeting people for the first time, you should already be making quite an impression. This is the time when they will decide whether to trust you or not. In the beginning, they will base their decision on the things that they observe about you.

You need to control other people's perception of you. Do this by copying how influential people dress, mimic how they speak, and exude confidence (without being obnoxious).

## Control What Other People Know About You

In the past, people will only get to know you if they saw you in person or if someone you know showed them your picture. Today, other people can proactively research who you are prior to meeting you. All they need to have is your name and they can easily search for your social media accounts.

Today, your social media accounts serve as a window your life. Modernization and technology have made it easier for this generation to know more about other people through the social media platform.

People can learn a great deal about you just by browsing your accounts. First, they can learn the people close to you by looking at your photos and your friend's list. They can also learn how you talk based on the way give comments or how you compose your status updates.

Other people can easily research what you do, what your interests are, what you like to, eat and a lot of other pieces of information that you care to share.

While most people take this tool for granted, you should expect that other people will look these accounts up when they meet you or expect to meet you for the first time. Knowing this, you should learn to control the information that people may find, especially by people who are not in your circle.

Instead of sharing random contents, show information that illustrates how influential you are. Share information that makes you seem an authority figure. If your occupation, for instance, commands respect, choose a profile picture where you are in your office uniform or in a suit.

## Aim to Make a Strong First Impression in Every First Meeting

In every first meeting, you should make sure to show people a strong and confident persona. People should get a positive good impression of you. Aside from your personal appearance, you could also create a strong impression by being in control of the interaction. Generally, you want to be perceived as a trustworthy, confident, capable, and dependable individual.

One of the ways to show that you possess these qualities is having a strong handshake. Most books will just tell you that a strong handshake should be firm and be done without hesitation. You should also control the handshake so that you will be more memorable to the person you meet.

Most people, for instance, only do two to three shakes before ending the handshake. You can take this opportunity show that you are in control by holding on for one more shake while asking the person you are shaking hands with a question. You can let go when the other person already answered the question. This shows people that you are comfortable with the first meeting.

Aside from the handshake, people also base their first impression of you on the way you interact. Ideally, you should talk in a manner that you are more comfortable in. You will be able to create a good first impression if you also make other people comfortable while talking to you.

You can do this by eliminating the dead air and awkward situations. You can easily do this with strangers by asking probing questions. In most cases, other people will carry most of the conversation once you find a topic that they are comfortable with.

A person's job, for example, is one of the most common topics that you can safely begin with. You can start by asking this question:

"What do you do for a living?"

After that, you can continue by asking an open-ended question like:

"That's awesome. How's that like?"

You can make variations of these questions according to the situation. The general goal is to make people talk openly about their jobs or whatever they are up to. This will usually allow you to carry a conversation without putting too much effort on it. Instead, you are letting other people do most of the talking while you just sustain the conversation by supplying more probing questions.

Another effective way to make people talk about something

they are passionate about is by asking them how to do certain things that are related to their expertise. If you are talking to a nurse, for example, you can say something like:

"I never actually learned how to spot the pulse on a wrist. Could you teach me how to do that?"

This may seem like a simple question, but it shows the person you are talking to that you are interested in their occupation and that you were paying attention when they were explaining what they did.

The skills in carrying first-impression conversations develop over time. For example, extreme introverts may not show confidence when they first interact. With practice though, they will be able to know the best practices in carrying out a conversation with confidence.

## Build an Image of Success

People generally want to follow people who are successful in their chosen field. People will want to interact with you more if they find that you can be a social asset to them.

Aside from your social media accounts and how others perceive you, people will also develop a good impression of you through the things your friends, family, colleagues, and even acquaintances say about you. You have to take note of these things – whether positive or negative comments.

You can learn this by talking with the people that you trust. For instance, you can ask a person that you trust what your reputation is among your circles. Tell them to be honest about it so that you can adjust any flaws in your image that will make it harder for you to persuade others in the future.

# Learn to use power words and positive language

Likability is an important trait of a persuasive individual. Even if you never got to close the deal with some people, they will consider going back to you in the future if they liked you upon meeting you.

One way to increase your likability is learning how to use powerful words that make the target audience feel good. When describing the offer, use strong words that will emphasize and even slightly exaggerate its positive features.

When complimenting those you are dealing with, use power words and phrases to make your compliments memorable.

Instead of saying that a person's new shirt looks good, you could say this:

"That's an awesome shirt. Where did you get it? I might just buy one for myself."

This statement creates multiple positive angles that you can use when working on the deal. First, it implies that you think that the other person has good taste. Second, you are also implying that you have something in common with the person you are talking to. When you practice your pitch or your sales spiels, look for opportunities where you can insert these power statements.

Another helpful technique: master the art of euphemism. People generally hate pessimists. They do not want to be surrounded by negative news and information all the time.

However, there are instances that the person involved is not aware that he is coming off negatively already. This impression may affect the outcome of the deal.

To prevent this from happening, you should make it a habit to use positive words even when you are saying negative things. The first step for most people is to remove profanities in their daily vocabulary. In most cases, profanity will not be taken positively by your target audience.

The next step is to build your vocabulary with positive words and idioms that will make negative statements sound more positive.

Instead of saying that:

"Our competitors have bad customer service."

You could say:

"Our customer service is better than most companies in the market today. We could try calling our customer support hotline now to check how well they actually perform."

With this statement, you turned a negative statement and an attack on another company into a positive note, while highlighting your own offer.

## Be Confident with What You are Saying and Be Firm

In the previous chapter, we discussed that the audience is using your confidence as one of the bases for their decision. To show them that you are confident with your offer, practice your presentation ahead. If you have a recorder, record your voice while you are practicing on persuading others. Afterwards, listen to your practice tapes and identify areas where you sound hesitant.

When you have identified these areas in your presentation, learn the reason for your hesitation. Sometimes, you may sound hesitant only because you lack practice. If this is the issue, you can easily remedy that by devoting more time to practicing.

Sometimes you may also sound hesitant when you have no confidence in the offer. Most people do not sound persuasive when they are second-guessing the effectiveness of their offer or if they are doubting their ability to deliver what is promised in the offer.

Making this doubt obvious when presenting your offer can be disastrous to your performance. The best approach to fixing issues with confidence is by improving the offer. Once the issues are addressed, you will be more confident while selling it.

However, at times, there may be nothing wrong with the offer. Instead, it is your perception of the product that shapes your attitude. In this case, changing what you believe about your offer will help you sound more convincing and confident. One way to do this is by focusing on the parts of the offer that you are confident of.

For instance, when persuading a friend to go to school, you may sound doubtful with your offer if you focus on the negative aspects of school. Instead of focusing on negativity, focus on the benefits your friend will get if he/she goes and finishes school.

By shifting your thoughts, you will also shift your attitude about your offer. Your positive attitude towards the offer will be translated into confidence in your presentation, thus making you sound more persuasive.

# 6 - Gaining Other People's Attention

Before you can start persuading others, you first need to get their attention. The longer you have other people's attention, the more opportunities you will have to get them to do what you want.

However, it could be a challenge to get their attention, especially nowadays when almost everyone has smartphones. You need to be creative for them to take a second look and listen to what you want to say.

There are a lot of things to do. Your actions will depend on what you are offering.

Here are some of the creative ways that you can do:

## Learn where the people you want to reach spend most of their time

When seeking the attention of other people, you are basically asking them for a few minutes of their time. The best time is when they are relaxing or when they don't have anything planned.

Study your target audience. Learn where they usually hang

out when they have time to spare. For example, your target audience watches a lot of TV, create a TV ad campaign. If they spend most of their time on their smartphones jut on-line advertisement options in social media.

## Use eye-catching colors in your messages

When you start reaching out to people, you should use eye-catching colors in your marketing materials. The best colors to use depend on the current trend in the market. Most books would tell you that colors like red and orange are most likely to get people's attention. While this is true in a general sense, they may become less effective when they are overused.

Aside from being eye-catching, the colors should "pop out" from all the other ads and promotional materials that your target audience use. When everyone is using a red "SALE" sign, for instance, you can have one created in gold with red print. Think of ideas for color combinations and test them out in the market.

## Use a compelling message

The colors that you use will not matter if the message in

your marketing materials does connect with the readers. The right message will depend on the type of people you are trying to invite. In a business setting, the best way to invite people to come to you is by creating a message that emphasizes the target market's pain point.

The pain point of the target market refers to the part of the business that they need to improve the most. If you want to get parents to buy vitamin supplements for their kids, for instance, you first need to identify how you are going to awaken their parental instincts. You can do this by mentioning a common problem among parents.

One example to consider is the kid's grades in school. To illustrate, schools are designed so that only a few students truly stand out. This usually includes the top ten students in the class. The rest are either labeled as mediocre or faring badly. You will be able to connect with the parents by creating a first line like this:

"Is your child mediocre?"

Most parents will answer yes in the back of their minds. You will also be able to connect even with the parents of the kids who are performing well. With this first message, you will create a feeling of concern in the minds of the parents. They will really assess their child's current standing in school.

Now that you have established the pain point of the parents, the next step is to create a second part of the message: one that establishes the solution to the pain. Assure the parents that what you offer will prevent their children from becoming mediocre.

In our example above, we are planning to vitamin supplements for kids. You can position your product so that it becomes a solution for the pain point that you've established.

## Call your target to act

Most ads and promotional materials make the biggest mistake in marketing, they do not call their target audience to act. You cannot just show an image of a person wearing your merchandise and expect buyers to proactively go to your store. People need a form of an invitation to go to your store or your office.

The third part of the message should tell your audience to go to you.

The content of the call to action button should be focused

on the goal that you want to achieve. If you have an online advertisement campaign and you want more people to go to your online store, your call to action statement should contain a message for them to go to your store and buy the advertised product. It would even be better if the ad comes with a link to the exact product they are interested in buying.

On the other hand, if your goal is to gather a list of prospective clients to avail of your services, you can also create a call-to-action statement that tells the reader which number to call.

Also, if the transaction should only be done at the site, your ad should contain the store's address and contact number, and instruct them to visit the store personally.

## Make it easy for your target audience to reach you

The call-to-action statement will only be effective the target audience can easily do it. The easier the process, the more effective your campaign will be.

You should think of the best way for your target buyers to

deal with you.

If you are running an online ad campaign, for example, you need to make sure that the process of signing up for your service or buying your product will take only a few steps. The signup form, for example, should only require basic information.

If you are trying to convince people to call you, request your telecom company to give you a number that is easy to remember. Most fast food delivery hotlines, for example, try to secure catchy phone number combinations. You should also do the same.

The best way to check if the process is smooth is by going through it yourself. After establishing your campaign, check if the contact channel is working well. If you are asking your audience to buy a product online, check if the checkout process of your product is working well by buying your own product yourself.

If you are asking your target audience to call a specific number, try to call that number with your personal line and act as a customer.

Testing them yourself allows you to assess everything personally. Making improvements will be easier, too, as you already know what works and what won't.

# If all else fails, contact your target directly

If casting a wide net (advertising) does not work in getting the attention of the people you want to persuade, the next best option is to contact them directly. Some companies still employ the door-to-door method of selling because it is the most effective. Additionally, companies still have their own telemarketers to offer products and services.

You should also make use of this direct tactic if it works for your product. The process will still be the same, only online.

When interacting with your target audience (in person or through the phone), try to establish a pain point first.

After establishing the pain point, position your product, service or offer as the solution. Then, ask the target to commit to an action.

Talking with the target directly is preferred by most negotiators because it gives them the opportunity for a two-way interaction.

Here are a few additional steps that you can take to make this process even more successful:

## Prepare for multiple pain points

Instead of creating just one general script for persuading your target, prepare different options. This will allow you to adjust your approach according to your target audience.

In our example above, you can adjust the pain point that you use depending on the type of parent you are dealing with. A single parent has a different set of problems compared to parents with a partner. Parents with many children on the other hand also have different sets of problems. Our hypothetical salesman can create different sales pitches according to the type of parent that he or she is selling to.

## Use probing questions

Probing questions refer to your inquiries that explore the problems of the person you are talking to. Doing so will allow your team in sales to know more about the potential customer.

In addition, they can also adjust the offer, whenever they deem it necessary. This will allow your staff to make a customized offer to the potential client. This will likely result in a successful persuasion process.

People like to feel important. Most potential customers would love to feel that they matter. Don't make sales pitches one after the other, you should learn to make the other person feel secured when they begin to strike a deal.

Also, if at the end of the conversation, the potential customer does not have a need for the product or service, he can ask for a referral instead.

For example, the sales staff is talking to the president of the PTA in the school. He could ask the potential customer if he could present the products to the other parents. If these propositions fail, the last step is to ask the target to provide at least one name as a referral.

## Understanding the Basics of Negotiating

When persuading people, you will eventually encounter different types of audiences. You will need to adjust the way you negotiate according to the types of people you are talking to.

Negotiating is the skill of interacting with another person or group to reach an agreement. The goal is for both parties to end up satisfied after the process. However, this is not always the case.

This happens because people usually want to push their luck when negotiating. The worst type of negotiator is one that is not willing to adjust his or her position to reach a compromise. This is where you will need the power of persuasion. One of the skills of a persuasive person is his or her ability to let other people see the situation from his or her point of view.

# 7 - The Essence of a Deal

A need for an agreement begins when one party has something that another party needs. A car salesman, for instance, has an inventory of cars that car buyers need. In this case, the exchange process is simple. The buyer just needs to put up the money to get the car or sign up for a financing plan to pay for the car with future income.

The process of negotiating becomes more difficult to deal with when the assets that are being exchanged do not have a predetermined value.

For example, in a labor case, the union of workers usually refuse to work in protest. The company in question usually wants their workers to go back to work. For that to happen, its management should meet the terms that the union offers.

In some cases, however, it is impossible for a company to meet the terms of the union without risking getting broke. In this case, each party has a different assessment of the value of the assets being exchanged. The only way for both parties to reach an agreement is if one or both adjust their terms for completing the deal.

Both parties need to arrive at an agreement where the company is not financially crippled and the union's terms partially satisfied. The negotiators from each side should reach a compromise. In the end, even if neither of the two parties was completely satisfied with the deal, the negotiation ensures that each will reap their own benefits.

## An Unfair Deal

When the negotiation skills of one of the representatives of the parties are below average, both parties will end up getting an imbalanced deal. This type of deal gives one of the parties a greater advantage.

In a sales arrangement, for example, an inexperienced buyer may end up buying a product at a price more expensive than its actual value. This results from the salesperson's superior knowledge of the product, the market, and the buyer's mind.

You do not want at the losing end of this kind of deal. If possible, you want to get the better part of the deal.

## Set Your Non-Negotiables

In each deal, the other side will try to tip the scales in their favor. A buyer of a property, for instance, may push their luck by lowballing the price. A complainant in a case may ask for an extremely high settlement amount.

These are just a couple of examples of how people try to push their luck in the negotiating table. You will be able to avoid being on the losing side of the deal by setting your non-negotiables and sticking to it.

Non-negotiables refer to the parts of your terms that you are not willing to compromise. One example of this is setting a minimum price for your products. By setting a minimum price, you are telling the buyers that you are willing to let go of the deal if you are haggled too much. This brings us to our next point:

## Be Willing to Walk Away

Before sitting down at the negotiating table, you should set a mindset that you are willing to walk away from the deal if your non-negotiable terms are not met. You will be in a bad position in a deal if the other party senses that you are unable to walk away from a deal.

In this case, people usually end up taking bad deals just to get the negotiation over with. By thinking and showing that you are willing to let go of the deal, you will force the other party to compromise.

You can show that you are willing to walk away from the deal by mentioning that you have other options. When buying a car, for example, tell the salesperson that you already visited another car lot and that you found a few that you already like. You can also say that you are there to check if they have a better offer.

By stating that you have other options, you are indirectly stating that you will walk away from the deal if the offers they have do not satisfy your needs.

# 8 - Persuade People Through Their Emotions

Many of us like to think that we make decisions with our minds. If you ask people how they made important decisions in their lives, they would give you answers like 'I used logic' or 'I asked for advice'. While we may use methods like these to a certain extent, the final decisions always boil down to how we feel about the decision.

Like when buying food, we often put a lot of thought on what to eat. If we were truly using logic, we would end up eating a salad every day. In most cases, we choose the types of food that we think will make us happy.

The only people who could resist the urge of buying delicious food over less savory ones are those who have greater goals, like people losing weight or athletes who aim to improve their performance.

Let's examine this phenomenon. Most people would say that these people who can resist delicious food and choose healthy ones are an exception to the rule. However, if we analyze these people closely, we can conclude that they are also using their emotions to make decisions. They feel so strongly about their goals that they are willing to give up the happiness they get from food.

It is extremely difficult for us to separate our emotions when making decisions.

## Awaking Other People's Emotions

When persuading people to follow your cause, you will need to consider the best emotions to tap. The best emotion to use will be based on the people with whom you are trying to work with and the product or service that you are trying to offer.

To know the emotions that will work best with certain types of people, try to think of their motivations. Parents, for example, are easy to profile because they will do anything for their children. When dealing with them, you can use emotions related to their children.

## Fear

A home security company may talk to parents and emphasize how dangerous their homes can be for their children. They may cite statistics and specific news reports of how children can be kidnapped on their way home from school and similar scenarios.

With this tactic, the presenter is using fear as the primary emotion to decide. Fear is effective in making people act. In the months and years following 9/11, for instance, news outlets unknowingly spread fear among millions of Americans by reporting about terrorist attacks twenty-four seven. The fear among the masses led to overwhelming support of the wars that followed.

## Happiness

Fear is not the only emotion you can use. In instances when people are not fearful, you may be labeled as pessimist if you keep on using fear as your tactic. To mix things up, you can also use other emotions like the promise of happiness when you are persuading others.

If you look at most print and digital ads, you will notice that companies tend to pair their products with smiling people. If their target market is teenagers, they may show good-looking teens smiling while using their products. In the same way, if their target market is young adults, they may show good looking girls (or boys) in their business attires smiling while holding the product.

The smile and the good looks of the models used by these

companies make the audience associate the product with the promise of being happy.

The promise of happiness, however, is usually best used when other (negative) emotions have been established. Negative emotions tend to increase the likelihood of success when persuading people.

## Envy

Aside from fear, you consider other negative emotions to start your negotiations with. Like, envy, which is another powerful emotion.

If you read motivational books in bookstores and online, you will notice that a lot of authors are writing about success. Most of the authors of these types of books start by bragging about their accomplishments. When you look them up using social media, you might observe them showing off their material acquisitions.

To the untrained eye, this behavior may seem like showing off. However, all these details are calculated efforts to create envy among the audience. When we see others happy with what they have, we tend to want the things that they have. This type of emotion can be observed often among children.

Children, unlike adults, do not have the capacity to filter their emotions. Because of their underdeveloped emotional skills, they tend to show negative emotions like envy in a direct manner.

For example, when a child sees another child with a toy, they cannot help but feel that they also want the same toy. Even though they probably have hundreds of pieces of toys at home, seeing other children playing happily makes them also want to try that specific toy.

Adults may have a better skill in filtering emotions. However, the feeling of envy also exists in their minds. The things that make them envious differ, though, based on what their values are.

A person who really wants to be successful will become envious when he or she sees others achieve success. A person, who is saving for a new home, may become envious when he sees some of his friends already achieving the goal he wants to achieve.

## Altruism

Altruism can also be a good emotion to tap, depending on the types of people you want to persuade. This emotion is best used when you are championing a cause that serves the underprivileged members of our society.

Charities for children might use sad photos of children to drive people to volunteer and donate. These organizations start with sadness and pity as their starting point. When that emotion has been established, they will offer for the audience a way to relieve that emotion by stating how they can volunteer or donate.

If your product or service offers this kind of value, you should certainly make use of the altruistic nature of people.

# 9 - Making Use of Emotions When Persuading People

Tapping on the emotions to persuade people has been used since the early days of human civilization. However, even today, only a few people know how to appropriately do it. This is partly because of the people who do know how to use this skill do not want others to learn about them. If the majority of the people know about them, these techniques will become less effective.

In this section, we will discuss how you to use this skill when persuading others:

## Define your target audience

To use this skill, you first need to learn about the people that you are about to influence. If you know what type of people you are dealing with, you will be able to adjust your strategy according to the situation.

To best prepare in employing this persuasion tactic, know their ages, at least. A high school teacher, for instance, needs to deal with adolescents. An insurance salesperson, on the other hand, needs to deal with middle-aged adults.

By learning about your target audience, you will be able to research on the things that they value the most. This information will give you a chance to create a pitch targeted to the values of your target. Only then will you be able to awaken other people's emotions.

## Learn about their values

The emotions of the people you deal with will depend heavily on the things or ideas they value most. The values of people vary depending on their culture and the period of life they are in.

When we were young, we always wanted to have fun and play. Children are easy to guess because they only want the things that make them feel positive emotions. They tend to be afraid of the things that lead to negative feelings. When persuading children, adults usually use the fear of punishment.

The idea alone of being punished scares most children into submission. Persons of authority, like parents and teachers, tend to become the primary source of power for children. Because children are easier to manipulate, they are protected by law against manipulation tactics. For instance, advertisements are not allowed to be targeted to children in most countries.

As children grow into adolescence, they begin to develop more complex thought patterns. Their values change according to the culture they are surrounded with. In western culture, teens tend to be surrounded by their peers most of the time. Because of this, the adolescent's values revolve around the approval of their friends.

For teens, negative emotions are usually associated with being humiliated in the group. The idea of being isolated from the group can be heartbreaking for most teens. They have this fear of other people laughing at them and they are at their most vulnerable when they don't belong to a group.

You can persuade teens by learning who they want to impress. Most of the time, they are attracted to the opposite sex. In some cases, they may want to impress the leaders of the group they belong to. A freshman, for example, may want to impress the older high school students.

On the other hand, negative emotions can be generated by emphasizing the possibility of being humiliated. You usually see this tactic in ads that promote beauty products.

For example, ads for pimple treatments and/or beauty soaps, target teens by emphasizing on the need to get rid (or prevent) acne because of the humiliation they could be subjected to. Upon injecting negative emotions to the target audience, the beauty product will be introduced and portrayed as the "savior".

As teens become adults, their values also change. From their peers, their focus is shifted towards career and life goals. This is when success tends to become the center of people's values. The way each person defines success, however, differs.

For an accountant, for instance, the meaning of success may be to be able to get big long-term clients. For teachers and other professionals in the academe, their values may revolve around increasing their rank in the universities where they work or contributing to the body of knowledge of their industry.

During the middle part of adulthood (the late twenties to early forties), people tend to start families. At this point, the concept of security and stability becomes important to them. They begin to fear difficult life events like sickness, difficult financial matters, or the possibility of raising unsuccessful children. All these are tied to their responsibilities.

Aside from this, their aspirations also make them vulnerable to the promises of happiness that comes with big-ticket purchases. To convince people in this stage of life, you need to emphasize how your product can help them achieve their dreams.

As adults advance in age, they tend to focus more on their legacy. At the later stage of adulthood, the number of responsibilities of a person tends to decrease. With this, they shift their focus to the things associated with later parts of life.

If they do not have enough saved yet, they tend to be focused on saving for retirement. If money is no longer an issue, they tend to shift their focus on their legacy. They value how they will be remembered when they are gone.

# Choose the correct emotion to tap based on your audience's values

Now that you know how to identify your target audience and their guiding principles and values, it's time to choose the emotion that will work best for them to accept your offer. As stated earlier in the book, it is best to start with negative emotions first because they are the most effective to tap into making people act.

To start, make a list of all the emotions that you can use for your offer. Go through the list of emotions above and connect them with the profile of your target market. Think of what lingering negative emotions your target audience has based on their life stage and their values. At the end of this step, you should be able to choose at least three emotions to use for your target audience.

# Align your offer as a solution to the negative emotion

Once the negative emotion has been established the next step is to offer subtly that you have a solution to the problem or issue. Your offer will be easily accepted when it is viewed as a solution to the problem. The goal is to create a promise of happiness and relief if they accept your offer. If you can establish this in your presentation, you will be able to have a higher chance of success in persuading others.

To support the promise of relief and happiness, you should present facts. Companies usually show statistical data about their offers. You will often see soap ads showing before and after pictures of their users. These are evidences that support your claim and it will appeal to the logical side of people.

By presenting these facts, you will be able to convince your target audience that they will be making the right decision if they take your offer. People react better if they are made aware of the benefits they stand to get. They do not like it if it they think that you played with their emotions to get what you want.

# 10 - Learning How Power Works in Society

Each community has strong leaders that make big decisions. In democratic governments, these are the people who are elected to office. In the schools, this may be the people chosen to become the president of the institution and the heads of each school department. People in powerful positions often have strong persuasion skills over the members of the society they have power over.

Have you ever wondered why these people have strong persuasive power? In this chapter, we will discuss the aspect of persuasion that is rooted in one's power or influence in society.

Eric Liu, an expert in the study of civic power, gave a TED talk on how power works in the society.

He stated that they are 6 types of forces that can give you the social power you need to influence and persuade people:

- Physical force

- Number of people

- Influential ideas

- State Action

- Wealth

- Social Norms

# Physical Force

Physical force refers to the use of force to make people do what you want. This source of power is considered the most primitive among the six. It is the source of power that rules the animal kingdom and it is the type that is most exploited in the less developed forms of society. In the modern world, we often see this force used by dictators and criminals.

While this source of power is effective in some forms of society, the other sources of power in the list prevents it to be as effective in civilized communities. Let's see how the other sources of power checks and balances the use of physical force.

# Number of people

The number of people supporting a person or an idea is also an important determinant of power in a society. This source of power has repeatedly been proven effective in multiple events in history. Governments have been created and destroyed through the will of the people.

In improving your own persuasive power, you should also consider increasing the number of allies you have. These are the people who support you and who are willing to act in your favor when the need arises. If other people with influence support you, their influence may also transfer to your own reputation.

## Influential ideas

An idea can also be a source of power if it gains support. For it to gain support, it should cater to the needs of the society. Many ideas that may seem like common today, drove the actions of the masses in the past. The abolition of slavery is the best example. It challenged the status quo, the powerful people, and institutions at the time.

Today, many ideas are gaining momentum. You do not need to waste a lot of time for no reason and brainstorm to create a new and revolutionary idea. Instead, to gain the support of the people around you and the persuasive power that comes with this support, you need to find an idea that you are willing to stand up for.

Politicians use this strategy all the time when they try to convince voters to choose them. They look for ideologies that get the most support from the masses and publicly show support to that ideology.

# State/institutional action

Power can also come from state action or the influence of the government. The government has the power to create rules in the form of policies and the organizational backbone to enforce those rules.

The policies created by the government can be used to control the resources in the society, empowering certain members of society. The checks and balances of a democratic government encourage that the policy-making of the government be used to empower the people.

This source of power can also come in governing bodies of smaller institutions. The people holding positions in these institutions are given the power and prestige associated with the post. In short, you will be able to increase your persuasive power if you are in a governing position in your community or society.

When improving your ability to persuade, you should consider the structure of organizations in your community. Learn the positions that will give you the most power over the people around you. Observe the people who are holding these positions now and how they are using the power that come with the post.

# Wealth

It is a known fact that wealth is also an important source of power. Wealthy people have more resources than other members of a society. They can use this wealth and transform it into allies in the society.

While wealth is not a prerequisite for becoming persuasive, it helps if you have it to back you up. You do not necessarily need to pay people to do the things you want. The mere reputation of being wealthy can increase your success rate in persuading people.

In developed nations like the US, wealth is a measure of one's productivity and value in society. If you are wealthy, other people assume that you have added value to the community.

This idea makes people with money and other important resources naturally easy to believe.

## Social Norms

Norms like cultural traditions and religious practices can also be a source of power. Norms govern how people think and how they act. They are the unwritten rules in the society. They may also be ways of doing things like the way we dress and the way we talk.

As stated earlier in the book, a person's power to persuade is greatly dependent on the way other people perceive him or her. Your ability to abide by the norms of a society will greatly affect your image.

In certain groups of people, being updated in the latest fashion, for example, will create a positive image for you. In certain subcultures, on the other hand, keeping up with the newest and most advanced gadget is the norm.

You want to understand how norms work in your own circles. You will need to understand how new trends are created so that you can harness these unwritten rules and preferred behaviors in persuading other people.

# 11 - Build your Power in Your Society

Aside from the tricks in this book, you will also become more successful in persuading others if you build your power in your own society. After this chapter, take the time to think about your own community. Think of the people who run the show and the kinds of power that they are using. Think of the sources of their power and the way they gain more power from these sources.

Lastly, think of the steps that you need to take so that you can gain more power in your own society. The more powerful and influential you are in your community, the stronger your persuasive power will be to its members.

## Exploiting the Human Mental Shortcuts

Our mind is designed for learning. When we observe something, our mind tries to remember it so that we can use that observation as a basis for future actions.

The mind will become overwhelmed as it consciously considers everything in the environment with each small decision. For this reason, it uses shortcuts to help us cope with each small task.

One of the shortcut mechanisms used by our mind is the stimuli-response reaction. The mind and body create an automatic action for certain stimuli that trigger it.

This is the basis of most of our habits. When we wake up, for example, we automatically do our morning routine without thinking of each step to take. In the same manner, we do the same things right after we arrive at work.

Right after we get home (stimuli), some of us will immediately throw our things in a receiving table and sit down on the couch to watch TV or connect to the Wi-Fi and use your laptop or smartphone. These are examples of routines that developed due to the stimuli-response mechanism.

This process works in many aspects of our lives. It even works in our mental processes and how we interact with people and things around us. When we enter a dark alley at night for example (stimulus), we may feel fear (response) based on the information that this is the kind of place where a crime can happen.

This stimulus-response mechanism happens every day and the people around us may exploit this survival trait for their own personal gain. Businesses around us for example may use a giant red sign on their windows that says "sale". To initiate the developed behavior of checking out anything that is on sale.

You should also learn the different automatic responses that people do. The best part about this mechanism is that you can readily observe them on people around you. Before we discuss specific stimuli-response examples that you can exploit when you are persuading people, let's first discuss how the process works.

## Breaking Down the Behavior

To learn about the stimulus-response mechanism, let's check out the behaviorist learning theories that were already established in the past. Ivan Pavlov is credited for one of the earliest experiments on behavior.

He tested a dog's reactions to stimuli associated with food. His experiment shows us that certain stimuli lead to specific sets of automatic responses. Today, we call this the classical conditioning theory.

Since then, many other behavioral psychologists added to what Pavlov started. For instance, BF Skinner formulated the operant conditioning theory. In this theory, Skinner suggests that a behavior will be constantly repeated when it could lead to a reward.

In this theory, Skinner suggests that the reward (or reinforcement) reinforces the behavior and it creates a mental pattern. When the mental pattern is repeated enough number of times (through drills), the stimuli-response mechanism is established.

To learn about how you can use this mechanism in persuading others, you should first learn its different components:

# The stimuli or the trigger

The trigger refers to the factor in the environment that will initiate and activate the entire mechanism to start. It could be a condition in the environment or the presence of a potential threat or reward that excites the subject.

# A shift in the mental and emotional state

The stimuli or trigger should change the emotional and/or mental state of the organism to make it act. The smell of food in the air, for example, will make the brain want to eat. A sight of attacking dogs, on the other hand, may trigger fear.

Chemicals in the brain create these emotional and mental states. One of the

Here are some of the common emotions or emotional states that you can use when developing your persuasion skills:

- Fear

- Interest

- Intrigue

## A predetermined response

The shift in the emotions or the mental state of an individual usually causes them to act. The action can be considered as the response. The response is created to lead to a sense of relief from the emotion or the mental state created by the trigger.

If the trigger creates fear, for example, it will initiate the fight or flight response. This is a well-documented response wherein the subject either stands his or her ground and fight or run away from the trigger and to move to safety.

# The reward or negative reinforcement

In most cases, the relief from the feeling of excitement created by the trigger is its own reward in the process. If a response leads constantly to the relief from fear, for example, that behavior will be repeated by the organism regularly. The removal of something negative to follow the correct behavior is called negative reinforcement.

Automatic behavior can also happen when a reward follows an appropriate action. For instance, buying something new creates a positive feeling in a person. This positive feeling makes us feel that we did the right thing. Most people with addictions crave the feeling that comes with their addiction. Like a shopaholic may crave for the feeling of buying something new.

# 12 - Shortcuts Exploited by Masters of Persuasion

Now that you know the process of automatic behavior and how they are learned, it's time to explore the different automatic behaviors common to humans.

## Our eyes are attracted to shiny bright colors

Have you ever wondered why most luxury items are designed to shine? Jewelry, for example, is polished until they shine in the light. Cars are rarely designed in matte. They are usually polished to shine in the sunlight.

People have a fascination with shiny objects. Anthropologists suggest that this fascination has its roots with one of our most basic survival instincts, our eyes are attracted to water. When walking in the wilderness, we usually see the water from a distance when hit by sunlight.

This causes water to shine from afar. After thousands of years of interacting with nature, our ancestors formed the habit of spotting shining objects from afar in the hopes that it could be a source of water.

This survival skill may not be as essential today that we have running water. However, our fascination for shiny objects and image has not left us. Today, we associate sheen and a smooth surface to things that are of high quality.

Application of persuasion:

If you want to get the attention of people, package the product you are selling in something shiny. When giving gifts, for example, a simple watch can become seem more expensive when it is polished to shine. People put more value on objects that shine. You can convince that an object you are selling is of high quality by adding a shiny finish to it.

# Price is associated with quality

Aside from shiny things, we also tend to associate quality with price. In a store full of merchandise, it is a common practice to assume that the most expensive item in there is also of highest quality. This is true in some of the most expensive possessions today, like electronic gadgets and cars. The more features they have, the higher their prices will be.

Unfortunately, this bias may be accidentally applied. This

usually happens when we buy things that we are not familiar with. In a coffee shop, for example, a person not familiar with coffee may assume that the items on the menu with the highest prices are the best quality coffee. Without asking about information, people are prone to making this type of bias.

Application of persuasion:

When persuading people, you can usually make products and services standout when you put a premium price on it. When you price the things or services lower than that of the competition, you are risking your products to be judged to be of lower value than other products in the market.

Ideally, you want to start by priding products high first. This way, when you put it on sale, people will assume that they are getting a bargain.

Store owners use this trick all the time. For products and services with prices that are not regulated by the government, merchants usually put them at a higher price according to the prices in the market. The high prices give the impression that the product us of high quality.

This is particularly effective when introducing a new brand in the market. Let's say you are a fan of sports shoes. You buy one new pair each month. You are familiar with all the brands in the market. Now, a new brand comes out. You are most likely to take the price of the shoe into consideration when assessing the value of the new brand.

## We put blind trust on testimonials

Aside from the two factors mentioned above, it is also common for people to base their assessment of the quality of a product or a service based on what other people say about it. As social creatures, humans depend on one another to survive.

If an ancient human told another that a tiger is lurking in the jungle, this will put the others on alert. If another human tells his tribesmen that a certain fruit is poisonous, they will also avoid the fruit.

Because of this, we generally trust the words of other people. The only exception is when the source of the information has the reputation of being deceitful.

With that said, companies often use this bias to convince

people into buying their products. A shampoo commercial, for instance, may hire a celebrity with long hair to promote their product. The fans of the said celebrity will follow her advice to buy the product. Some would even say that the long hair of the celebrity is the proof the product is effective. These lines of reasoning, however, are false.

The hair of celebrities usually gets more treatment than that of a normal person. It usually takes hours of preparation before stylists get their hair just right for events. The hair that we see in print and video ads are usually edited to bounce and shine the way they do.

Most us know this and still choose to ignore it. People generally take the shortcut and trust that the celebrity is telling the truth about the product.

Application of Persuasion:

When persuading people, you will often find it hard to make them believe you if the idea, product, or service you are offering is new. It will be easier for you to make people believe you if you have someone of good reputation back your word.

When creating a presentation for your product, service, or

idea, for example, make it a point to include the testimoni-
als of people who used them in the past. By showing that
other people are using what you are offering, you will be
able to give social proof of its effectiveness.

This method is often used on websites like Amazon. People
generally trust the user-generated review systems on this
website. They trust what these reviews say even though they
do not know the people giving the reviews.

# We see the first price mentioned as our baseline for haggling

When we are talking about price, the first price mentioned
is called the anchor price. It is called the anchor price because it sets the amount as the baseline in the mind of the
buyer and the seller.

Let's say you are negotiating a settlement and the person on
the other side of the negotiating table says that they will
settle for $100,000. From the moment the price is men-
tioned, both parties will just be hovering around this price.
Your next offer will always be affected by the first price
mentioned.

In the negotiating table, the first person to mention the price has the power to set the anchor. When persuading other for a price, make sure that you control this factor. In situations where the product has no asking price, the first one to make an offer at a lower price than you, is willing to pay for the product.

If you want to buy a car from a friend, for example, you can offer $1,000 for it even if you intend to pay $1,500. By setting a low anchor price, you will have more room to haggle with the price.

This brings us to the next point...

## Moving your price is a sign of defeat

When persuading someone, we often want to make them feel that they've made the right decision. It will be easier for you to persuade people if you master the art of controlling their emotions. In the previous section, we discussed the idea of the anchor price, now that you have set it, the next step is to ask for a counteroffer from the other person.

A negotiator with a sharp mind will not allow the anchor price to affect his or her counteroffer. Most people you deal with though, are more likely to base their next offer on the anchor price. When they do, this means that you have control over the negotiations.

At this point, you already have the anchor price and the counteroffer. Most people would just meet the other person halfway and get the deal over with. It is wiser to move the price just a fourth of the distance between the two prices.

If the anchor price is $1,000 and the counteroffer is $2,000, your next offer should $1,250. By moving your price up, this will signal the other person that you are willing to adjust to reach a price that both parties can be happy with.

By not meeting the price halfway, you are giving yourself more room to negotiate if the other person decides to haggle some more, which is often the case with experienced negotiators.

After they make another offer, you may now meet them halfway. By moving your price up, you are feigning weakness. You are showing the other party that you moved your price up for them. By doing so, you make them feel that they won the negotiation.

This trick is often used when a master negotiator is dealing with inexperienced people. The master negotiator makes the other party think that they are the ones who decided to close the deal, not knowing that the master negotiator is in control the whole time.

## Our eyes are attracted to unusual colors

Our eyes are amazing organs. They are designed to receive reflections of light from objects and relay the information it gathers to the brain. To make it effective, the eyes and the brain have learned tricks on how to focus the attention on just a few things.

With the thousands of things around us at one time, our eyes work with our brain to classify everything fast. This method of classifying things subconsciously is a survival trait that we got our ancestors. In the wild, our ancestors' eyes needed to be sharp in spotting unusual colors.

## We trust uniforms too much

The way people dress is also a strong basis for our judgments towards them. The first time we meet a person, we make over a hundred judgments about that person. When making these judgments, we use shortcuts to make the process faster. A person's way of dressing becomes one of the main factors that we consider when making these judgments.

With that said, the uniform can be an important tool when making a good first impression. When you meet with people when you're wearing a uniform of authority, they are likely to have more respect for you, than when you are dressed like the others.

When you are trying to convince people, you should dress the part of the negotiator. Let's say you are trying to close a deal with a group of businessmen, you should not negotiate just wearing a regular shirt and a pair of jeans. The people you are talking to will treat you according to the way you dress.

Instead, you should dress up the way the other business people dress. If they are always in a corporate attire when meeting with you, you should do the same. Your attire sets the level of authority that the other party should treat you.

When negotiating, we often need people of authority to speak for us. When presenting a product, for example, we may need our team of engineers to explain how the product works. When presenting medical products like a drug medicine, you may need to have a doctor present the product so that the technical parts of the product will be explained thoroughly.

The people you work with to explain the product will also be able to benefit in wearing the right attire. In their case, however, they are more likely to benefit if they wear clothes fitting to their occupation. By wearing their uniforms, they will set the proper first impression to the people they are presenting to.

## Faking it with uniforms

Sometimes, you may need to pretend that you are someone you are not. For instance, a guy presenting his app to a venture capitalist may need to show them that he is a serious businessman rather than just a programmer working all day in front of his computer. That person can improve the first impression he makes by wearing a business attire, rather than his usual jeans and hoodie getup.

# 13 - The Rule of Reciprocation and The Need to be Consistent

In the previous chapter, we talked about some of the biases that people use as shortcuts when making quick decisions. When used masterfully, you can use those biases to increase that likelihood of persuading another person.

In this chapter, we will turn to another strategy of obliging people to act favorably to your goals. Master of persuasion uses this method all the time. It's called the rule of reciprocation.

## Definition

This rule suggests that people are generally inclined to return favors and to repay debts. This phenomenon has been observed by anthropologists and sociologists in many societies.

A tribe in one of the Pacific islands, for instance, would travel thousands of miles to another tribe just to offer gifts, without asking anything in return. However, the effort is considered an offer of to form an alliance between the two tribes. If the tribes are already allies, it is a way to keep the alliance intact.

# 13 - THE RULE OF RECIPROCATION AND THE NEED TO BE CONSISTENT

As human society became more complex, we had to have rules on how resources were shared among the members of society. Relationships in a society are forged when we abide by these rules.

A person, for example, may watch over his neighbor's son while the other is dealing with an emergency. He does this only with the assumption that his neighbor will do the same for him. This process is common in close communities.

When one deviates from this rule, the society usually brands that person with a negative label. People who do not give back are called names such as selfish, stingy, or inconsiderate. To avoid these labels, people generally abide by the rule of reciprocity.

Application of persuasion:

The task of persuading others will be much easier when you use the rule of reciprocity to your advantage. You can do this by raking up social points among the people around you. Many people around you have been doing this all their lives. You see people who are so nice to other people and who are so generous with their time and money. Other people would come to their aid when they are in need.

If you haven't built this kind of reputation yet in your community, don't worry, you can still start today. By actively building your relationships with people based on the rule of reciprocity, you can decide who you can give favors for. This is essential especially if you have limited resources.

Before we discuss what you need to do to build your social points, let us first talk about the guidelines that you need to follow when you are collecting favors:

# Try to limit the cost of your gifts or favors.

This rule does not have a 100% chance of success. Some of the people you interact with, will not return the favor. Because of this, make it a rule of thumb to minimize the cost when you are helping someone.

This will ensure that you will build your social points without sacrificing your own resources. If you need to give people something of value, it should be time. People are more likely to remember you when you spend a lot of time with them.

# Think of the possible favors that you may ask people when you do something for them

It will be easier for you to justify your generosity and your altruism if you think of the benefits that the person you are helping can give you. When doing this, consider all the factors. Most people would just the financial help or the influence of the person when helping others. When you do it, also consider the less obvious ways that the person will be able to help you in the future.

One way to do this is by considering a person's job. Professional advice can be expensive if you go to strangers. When you ask someone whom you helped before for their professional advice, they will help you especially of the advice will not cost them anything.

## Label your offers as gifts

When giving something to the people around you, label them as 'gifts'. When you label them in any other way, they may mean a different meaning. For instance, if you label them as promotions, the person receiving them may not feel as special for receiving them.

They may also think that you just gave them something that your business or office is giving away. The same goes for commonly used marketing terms like giveaways, add-ons, or free items. While these things are designed to catch the attention of people, they do not create the feeling of giving back.

Instead, make the idea of your offer more personal. An ice cream company training their staff to give free samples, for instance, could tell their customers to use personalized lines.

For instance, they could use the following line when they only have one customer:

"As a gift, I'll an extra scoop just for you. If you want some more, the product will be available all year round in..."

The next time the recipient of the gift sees the product, they will buy it even if they do not need it.

Here are some of the things that you can start doing to start racking up your social points:

# Attend all social events that you are invited to

It is common for people to avoid social events nowadays. Many introverts sometimes fail to show up in events they are invited to for the smallest of reasons. Most of us see these events as unimportant.

However, if you want to become a master of persuasion, you need to consider that the people who invited you to these events may take offense if you miss it. If you committed to going to a social event, always keep your word, and go to that event.

You should actively go to events that show support. Wakes and funerals are a prime example. When an immediate family member of a person you know dies, make it a point to go to the wake or the funeral and show your support to your friend. Even if you do not know that person well, the family members will remember it if you show up in their time of grief.

Another important event is when someone is staying in hospitals. Nowadays, people take health concerns for granted because health concerns are rarely serious. You will be easily remembered if you took the time to visit people in the hospital. You can also bring something for the family to enjoy.

# Do not refuse people asking for favors

Every now and then, people will come to you for favors. This is a good opportunity to for you to stack up on social points. You must not let this opportunity go to waste.

When people come to you to ask for a favor, find a way to help that person. If you cannot personally help him or her, make it a point to find someone you know who can help them. If you put some effort in helping others, the majority of people you help will repay you in the future.

A trick to prevent your favor from being forgotten:

It is common, however, for people to forget favors. When granting favors for others, make it a point to make the experience memorable. After granting the favor, you can mention that they could repay you by buying you a cup of coffee. You can then make sure that they never get to buy you that cup of Joe.

When you meet that person in the future, remind him that he or she still owes you a cup of coffee, again avoiding opportunities for that person to buy you one. Mention it to them playfully so that they will not be offended or annoyed with your humor. This way, they will always remember that you were there when they needed you.

In other instances, you may also start small talk regarding the subject. Let's say you helped a friend in getting his son to a good school. The next time you meet a few years later, you should mention the favor with the intention of asking about how his son is doing in his school.

## Make use of social media

Nowadays, it is easier to broadcast your altruism to the people you know: through social media. Take photos of the time you spend helping other people who ask for favors. This way, you will be able to let other people know how helpful you are.

Letting other people know about the small things that you do for others will help you build a reputation. Even the people you do not help will consider giving you favors in the future because they know that you do the same for them if they came asking for help.

# Sweeten deals by giving gifts before negotiations

When you are asking a person for something, make it a point to come in person rather than talking on the phone. When you visit, be sure to bring something as a gift. When visiting a grandmother who has a linking towards cats, for instance, you can bring cat shaped cookies with you. It does not need to be expensive. As the saying goes, 'It's the thought that counts'.

You should also adjust your gifts according to the types of people that you are dealing with. When meeting with a person in the corporate world, for instance, you could give a gift that fits their interest. If you see that the person that you need to deal with likes to go biking on the weekends, for example, you could buy them a gift about biking.

When giving gifts, timing is also important. Ideally, you should give the gift before the meeting. If you do not know the person, this will start the meeting in a good way. You should then follow the gift-giving a short conversation.

# 14 - The Need to be Consistent

Few qualities make a person more dependable than consistency. We want the people around us to be consistent with their words and actions. We also want to look dependable, consistent individuals.

The need to be consistent is even greater after we make an important decision. This need can be seen among people who made a purchase. Right after a person made an important purchase, he immediately sees the product he bought to be superior to others in the market. After buying a car, for example, most people would remind themselves of the great features of the car that made them buy it in the first place.

In addition, they try to avoid the car market altogether. Most of them would say that they do this because they no longer need to buy a car. However, another reason they do this is probably because they do not want to see other cars on the market that would make them doubt their choice. They want to consistently believe that they made the right decision.

## Understanding the behavior

The need to be consistent is so common that it can be seen

in everyday decisions. One a person decides to do something, you can count on him or her, following through with that decision.

One reason for this is that most people do not want to be wrong. We try to justify each of our decisions. Hence, it is so difficult to convince other people to change their minds once they have decided on something. It is easier to persuade people who haven't made their decisions yet.

## Application of Persuasion

When persuading people, you can easily use this pattern of behavior by creating a commitment trigger. A commitment trigger refers to a small commitment that you arrange with your target. For instance, instead of setting up a sales meeting, you can say that you just want to have lunch with your target. It is easier to have your targets agree to free lunch than a sales meeting.

Afterwards, you can set up other commitment triggers. Let's say you are offering your company products to be sold in a retail shop in your town. Tell the target to try selling only a small amount of product. It will be easier for them to commit if the offer is small. If the product sells, the target will be forced to follow through and be consistent. They will need to continue selling more of your products.

In contrast, they may have never agreed to put your products on their shelves if you offered them to sell a large amount from the beginning.

# 15 - Conclusion

Thank you again for buying this book!

I hope this book was able to help you to understand and develop your persuasion skills.

The next step is to start working on your skills and apply them to your own profession. Start by practicing with smaller persuasion projects. Schedule a meeting with your boss and persuade them that you will do a good job if you are promoted. Persuade your kids to do better in class.

As you improve your skills and you develop a wider skill set, try taking on bigger persuasion projects. Over time, you will become a master in persuading the people around you.

Thank you and good luck!

# Thank You

As we reach the end of this book, I want to say thanks for reading this book.

I want to get this information out to as many people as possible. If you found this book helpful, I would greatly appreciate you leaving me a review. This helps others find the book as well.

# Disclaimer

This document is geared towards providing exact and reliable information in regards to the topic and issue covered. The publication is sold on the idea that the publisher is not required to render an accounting, officially permitted, or otherwise, qualified services. If advice is necessary, legal, financial, medical or professional, a practiced individual in the profession should be ordered.

This information is not presented by a financial or medical practitioner and is for entertainment, educational and informational purposes only. The content is not intended as a substitute for professional medical advice, diagnosis, or treatment. Always seek the advice of your physician or other qualified health care provider with any questions you may have regarding a medical condition. Never disregard professional medical advice or delay in seeking it because of something you have read.

The information provided herein is stated to be truthful and consistent, in that any liability, in terms of inattention or otherwise, by any usage or abuse of any policies, processes, or directions contained within is the solitary and utter responsibility of the recipient reader. Under no circumstances will any legal responsibility or blame be held against the

## DISCLAIMER

publisher for any reparation, damages, or monetary loss due to the information herein, either directly or indirectly.

Last Updated: 25.Dec..2017

Printed in Great Britain
by Amazon